The Shadowed Rose
That Grew From His Shine

Book Interior Design

by

J. Michael Shoemaker

Cover Image

by

M. Roth from Pixabay

The Shadowed Rose
That Grew From His Shine

By
Malcolm Leroyce

Published by

Liberated Miracles, LLC
Aiken, South Carolina

www.MalcolmLeroyce.com

Thank You

I must begin from the heart by saying, faithfully and honestly, thank you to the Most High, for all of creation is good. I continue to give thanks to all of the angels that are and ever have been concerned over thee.

I'm forever thankful to my parents, Leroy and Janette, for their uni-factional love which brought me forth. Much love for my siblings, Cheryl, DMack, Dno (RIP), Toot, Delton, and to my entire family tree from day one, for helping to ignite my fire from within that burns brighter each day. An abundance of thanks and one love to the humanity Fam and to the community, North Aiken, South Carolina.

And, a very special Big Ups to J. Michael Shoemaker for cranking up my drive.

Last but not least, I would like to thank Mr. Steve Harvey for your humorous and inspirational morning show which has been a huge motivation for me to take this leap of faith (J.U.M.P.)

Contents

The Shadowed Rose
That Grew From His Shine

By
Malcolm Leroyce

Chapter 1
Earmalc

The Shadowed Rose That Grew From His Shine

Dedicated to One Nation

I never had much but an established heart full of grace.
And a bedroom in the projects, that I shared with my brothers all the days.
A couple of outfits that I had to rearrange on the daily to look cool.
Until being pointed out by bully laughter,
                    that Friday morning in high school.
Thou very thankful, indeed poverty is what made me strong.
With honored grades, nothing really mattered, because,
                    I knew I was built to last long.
But with the around and around moving in this town,
                    made it hard to settle in.
From side to side, from time to time, we had to go,
                    making it hard to keep a friend.
But, what was last is meant to be first,
                    so, I patiently waited and wanted for nothing.
Dedicating my focus on God's will, cleaning up my act,
                    because I know he's coming.
I was blinded for the longest, on how to be a part of this nation,
                    born from a sick society.
For they are a rebellious house, loving to lie,
                    which taught me unrighteousness quietly.
Now, with my every ambition, I learn, blossom and teach,
                    those willing to listen, to what's been taught through me.
Doing my Jesus thing, to ease the peoples' pain,
                    giving light for even the blind to see.
I don't regret where I'm from, because, I made it through my trials,
                    making it exciting, to now know who I am.
Being the descendant of the children of Israel, the Godly seeds,
                    seeing myself as the charm of the humanity, Fam.
I am that shadowed rose that grew from his shine,
                    which took me twenty-nine years to climb.
Enlightened by Mr. Shakur and those who enlightened him,
                    and future more, the Lord who's always on time.

Shine Time

Is It Me?

Is it me, that causes the hell on Earth that walks with me through life?
Or, is it me, that causes the heavenly thoughts,
which, helps me sleep at night?
Is it me, that ran my family away, or, is it me,
that taught my family to pray?
Is it me, who my kids look up to now,
or, is it me who doomed my kids to be Hellbound?
Is it me, the people love, or, is it me, the people hate?
Is it me, who needs to migrate, or is it me who needs to stay?
Am I the reason, that I have no friends,
or, is it just that impossible for them to be?
Is it me, that shows love just a little too much,
when this world today, ain't surrounded by peace?
Is it me, that laughs, when I should be crying,
and, is it me, that lived at times of dying?
Is it me, making it hard for myself to focus on me,
being heavenly sent and chosen?
Or, is it me, being careless, not even trying, to apply my status,
when my mental is open?
Why me, I ask, being God's child,
blessed with the umbrella for the pouring rain?
Being the lonely stoner, in a lonely corner,
granting access to those going against the grain?
Is it me, the one with a spot already in heaven,
or, is it me, the one that one day just might be a reverend?
Or, is it me, just fooling myself, awaiting hell's pits, knowing,
I am half devilish, because positive and negative do coexist?
Confused I am, that I do know, manifesting,
I get my chance, in this life, to put up a high score!
Could I be the comforter that has come, the one,
that will place smiles upon their face?
If so, I got to start with myself,
because, it hurts to carry around this poker chase.
Is it just me, with a wish, for the ones I love, to be on one accord,
like a school of fish?
Is it just me, wanting to be the genie,
granting every wanted Aladdin's wish?
I think it is me, as a matter of fact, I know it is.

Am I Really Free?

They say it is the Land of the Free,

                        but, all I see, is the Land of the Lie.

Got young brothers seeing ten, twenty to life,

                               causing mothers to cry.

Am I free enough, to become successful within the blink of an eye?

Or, are we free to harm ourselves, with corruption, and die?

My country has no codes to live by,

                    except, for the words of God to stay right.

But, while they generalize the brains,

                        it makes it hard to even play our plight.

Am I truly free, though my body is locked up at times?

I'm asking, because, what freedom means to me, is peace in minds.

The Seeking Of Liberation.

The Finger Pointer

If it's one thing I can't stand, it is being accused for something I didn't do.
Those that aim to false claim, you got it coming to you.
Pointing the finger at me, leaves three pointed back at who?
Whoever you trying to place the blame on, it's really what you do.
Be a man and take a stand, for your own consequences.
Keep it real with yourself, you can't play both sides of the fences.
Be careful with the relentless, if they did do it, you still need to hush up,
because snitching on real Gs, gets you lost when touched.

Mind your Business

I Might Be a NIGGA

I might be a Nigga, never ignorant, getting goals accomplished.
But, I ain't yo nigga, which, is ignorance and dumbness.
Don't play me bout my color, because, I'm raised from the ghutta.
I'm an intelligent young man, so, please, address me as 'Brother.'
I done suffered enough of the nick picking, and the finger pointing.
To overstanding how to rebuke, and keep my household anointed.
So, you can call me a Nigga, but, I'm still a man with a heart.
And, yea, I might be the left behind, but, I'm way past start.

My Eye Stay Jumping

My eye stay jumping, what could this mean?
Is it something good, about to happen, because, I need it seen?

My eye stay jumping, what would this be?
Is it a happy congregational conversation, somewhere based on me?

My eye stay jumping, what should I say?
Is it somebody looking for me, wanting to see me today?

My eye stay jumping, and its aggravating.
Is it all of the above, or, just the lurkers waiting and hating?

I Need an Answer.

Heavy Pressure

I can't sleep, it's hard to eat, and it hurts to speak.
This constant battle with sin, makes me want to give up,
but, that's not me.
I'm trying to do right, but, things stay going wrong.
I know y'all readers out there saying,
this nigga going through the same old songs.

Of course, when the pressure is on, it's a hit.
Who's doing the swinging? I don't know,
but, I wish it was me that they'll miss.
It's hard to think straight, and I just lost my peace.
Now, I don't like anybody,
so, everybody better stay out of my reach.

How can I clearly pray to God, with hate in my heart?
How can I have a victorious ending,
when, I don't even know a way to start.
I'm ready to erupt, volcano style, and release this build up.
But, I ain't even got a girl in this world, that truly loves me.
Am I that fucked up?

I ain't got no time for conversation, I'm now in isolation.
Ready to bomb first on anybody,
while, signing applications for Satan.
Seriously, what is love,
when, the whole world lying, directly to my face?
Humans are the most conniving creatures.
Make way, before, I catch me a murder case.
This pressure is too heavy, to bear on my own,
somebody, come take it away.
Lord, I need your help, I know you hear my cry.
Please, answer my call today.

My Heartbeat

I think my heart just skipped a beat,
I'm losing my cool.
I think my heart just skipped a beat,
My religion is lost too.

I know my heart ain't on beat,
There's hate on my mind.
I know my heart ain't on beat,
I'm lost in time.

My heart hasn't been the same,
Since I changed my game.
My heart hasn't been the same,
With extra madness on my brain.
Maybe, my heart does deserve a reliever,
I'm in need of a thug's stimulation.

My heartbeat craves peace,
I'm in need of a thug's medication.

Pass the 'lye' my way.

No Restraints

Now, as the game recycles, the elders rest their hands,
                  while the younguns enter, as wild cards.
With no understanding, of the rules of this vicious sport,
             just running loose, without keeping up their guards.
There is no respect, shown for those that been,
        they just try to find a vacant spot, that they can fit in.
With no control over their goals, just knowing how to give, grab, and go,
        you can expect, they'll fade away, like the wind.

You see, the elder had wiser parents,
        that taught them how to say no, to certain things.
So, there was always a time they knew, how to negotiate in the game.
But, the youngun got youngun parents, that wasn't taught correct,
        so, they don't know how to teach.
Then like a horse with no leash, no one can hold them back, from headfirst,
        kicking up dust in the street.

There are no restraints in the morals of today, no mutual feelings involved,
        it's like it's every man for themselves.
Now, that old game of, "I Declare War," done became reality,
        while, they switching up the cards, that was dealt.
And, the cycle only gets rougher,
      because, when they come to handing over their throne,
        the next in line is more wicked.
And, to be specific, there'll never be restraints again,
      in the game of the illegal hustle up, for the fool's meal ticket.

The Game has Gone Sour

The Push

When one door shuts, another door will open,
>> you, just have to maintain focus.
If you do what you did, you'll get what you got,
>> so, it's time to recognize your comings and goings.
Rough times will put you down, grounded but able,
>> thank God for motivational speeches.
From people who do care, to see me reach my goals,
>> instead of gold digging money sucking leeches.
I often find myself trapped in hidden situations,
>> which, only makes me go hard in the paint.
Pushing me past the limits, just to see my cans,
>> when, I find myself saying, "I can't."
There's a must, I climb, my family deserves to shine,
>> though, we already come with a glow.
Until my feet reach the peak, and my pinnacle's beneath me,
>> I'm never letting this new push go.
>> From a starting kit,
>> to getting known,
>> to word of mouth,
>> to a job well done,
I'll be getting at them top shelf digits.
With my Loyal unit, repping, Liberated Miracles,
>> all on one accord, praising the Lord,
>> As we,
>> Get,
>> Get,
>> Get It!

Can't Stop, Won't Stop!
Just, Gotta Keep On Pushing!

Water

Water is a part of everything.
It covers seventy percent of the Earth.
It is also sixty percent of your body.
And, has been that way, and then some, since your birth.
It's the reason being, why eight cups a day, is needed in life.
Like gasoline for a car, it gives you drive, on sight.
It's such a wonderful feeling, it enhances the brain.
It Lubricates the body, to score high, in this game.
You see, the game of life, is meant to be, played by the rules.
So, treat yourself to some water, instead of the fading, from brews.

Put it in your diet and try it.

Fruits & Vegetables in my Bowl

And, God said, "Behold," I have given you every herb bearing seed,
     which, is upon the face of all the earth.
And, every tree,
          which, is the fruit of a tree yielding seed,
                    to you, it shall be for meat.

Meat, meaning a necessary thing, not dead animals.

     Lets start over, and eat healthy, and live life longer.
          An undefiled body, will only make you stronger.
          Don't get it twisted, there are many vegetables,
          You won't live in hunger.
               Reconsider, and feel the beauty.
               Or, eat the dead, and be, "A soon to be goner."

Live as an eagle and eat alive.
Dead weight only holds you down, fly high!

Eleven More Minutes

The pain is real, the hurt is undoable, I'm in need, of some relief, like now.
I've been wanting to quit, but, can use one last hit,
                steady going, against my resought vows.
Life's an emotional blow of wind, on its daily course,
                and, of course, it got me feeling a Newport.
Cool? My friend just pulled a pack out of his pocket,
            and, once I ask him for one, for sure he'll support.
True indeed, I sparked the question,
            and, then received a form of destruction.
My lady friend hates the smell, so, at times, our 'we' be suffering.
It's beating down my health, though, I crave its response.
I must come to a point, where my needs outweigh my wants.

One would say, "It doesn't matter,
      those, will be the eleven minutes of my gray old hospital bed days."
Some would say, "You got to die of something."
And, most would say, "I know, but, I'm quitting after this pack."

The body is a precious thing.
Take some thought time out, and think about it.
Life is truly the greatest thing, to ever posses.
Learn to Love, to live it, and then Live.
Cold turkey vitalizes the prosperity.

Family Feuds

A family that prays together, stays together.
But, a family that hates each other, wasn't made for each other.
We say thank you, we say you are welcome,
                we invite us over, to make things better.
The bondage of Love, we express, can grow to a whole other level.
The bloodline will remain, teaching our kids to be clever.
Hosting our church at home,
              because, home is the way we keep out the devil.

Though we gone fight, or, we gone feud, fo sho that's just what families do.
But, I guarantee tomorrow, we'll laugh about it over a blunt and a brew.
We never take matters personally; we take heed of our statements.
At times, we be out of order, not realizing the shit we be saying.
Indeed words hurt more than blows, to the mind.
We must think, before we speak, because true Love is hard to find.

Some grudges last for years, until caskets are closed,
              causing everlasting tears.
But, being raised as wild adolescents,
           makes it complex, to respect our peers.
Let's let, bygones be bygones, for forgiveness is music to thy soul.
I'll Love to see my kids, have grand kids, of their own,
           meaning, together we'll have had to grow old.
The feuds must stop, or, at least give it a try.
Because, a cry is not a cry, until you see a Loved one die.

Family Matters

When I Die

My body was not built to last, so, I've prepared for my separation.
Once my soul moves on, it shall remain in a place, full of celebration.
So, up until that moment, I have no time to sleep.
On my day-to-day mission, grinding mines for keeps.
Staying alert, in order to leave my offspring, plenty of bling.
To the world, I will leave my last album titled, "The Will of My Aim."
To my moms, I'll leave my heart, pure enough to see God.
To my pops, I'll leave my props, and my favorite rod.
To my sisters and my brothers, I'll leave my companies for no struggles.
To my nieces and my nephews, I'll leave my learns to bubble.
To all my hustling cousins, I'll leave my spirit to hustle dozens.
To my ghutta Comrades, I'll leave my weaves from trouble.
To my female friends, I'll leave my one last kiss.
To all those that persecuted me, I'll leave my ass to kiss.
When it's all said and done, rest me in peace, like a Pharaoh,
still standing, because, the only time I laid flat,
was to rest my bone marrow.
As I said before, I'll sleep when I die, so, at my funeral,
party like it's September tenth, without a cry.

*A*men...

Down Hill From Here

It's September Fourteenth, and I'm upstairs reading my bible.
Not knowing at the same time, I'm being plotted on by a rival.
Their creepy crawling sounds, fair warned me of the enemies approach.
So, while they was trying to force entry,
                    I was lead to safety by God, my coach.
They trapped themselves as the police arrived,
                    straight trapped inside of my house.
With no way of seeing freedom, they finally came out,
                    and then, I heard a sound go "POW!"
That's when it stopped, they all got locked, dumb asses shot at the cops.
To make a long story short, I got evicted from my spot,
                    and then, it was on to the next block.
Back home with moms, wasn't what I planned,
                    especially coming from my own, being my own man.
A tough pill to swallow, and too ashamed to borrow,
                    so, I had to deal with it the best way that I can.
It didn't last long, with that same old song,
                    those old fights, reappeared with my father.
I repacked and shipped out, played the couch at my homey's,
                    while praying for a better tomorrow.
Shortly after that, it was time to move again,
                    my so-called friend, found himself a girlfriend.
I just lost my job, due to the lack of transportation.
On top of that, I'm down to my last ends.
This snowball effect is killing me to think,
                    and homeless definitely ain't an option.
At times I hate I came up in the struggle,
                    as if, I should have been put up for adoption.
Dammit man, this wasn't part of the plan, I reckon it's time to call Dbo.
He's my guardian angel, known for uplifting my spirit,
                    and that's why I call him my Big Bro.
I'm getting tired of the suffering. I'm getting tired of the pain.
Thou his roof umbrellaed me through the pouring rain, and then it came.
February Fifteenth, my little man's birthdate, and I'm feeling very sane.
Until I got hit by the blue lights, with a warrant on my name.
O shit, now its jail time I got to do.
Damn if it ain't been downhill since the home invasion,
                    but, it's a must that you read my part two.

Chapter 2
Thinking of You

The Bandaged Bell

Dedicated to: My Daughter, Liberty

Up until nine twenty two, single O'seven, there was no Liberty,
thou, the bell that stood, held a crack.
Then along she came, from my very own name,
representing my aim to give back.
Her mother was pure at the time, she conceived,
so, the fruit of the tree is good.
Give her time to overstand, who she is in this world, and she'll liberate,
starting fresh in the hood.
She is a Virgo like me, her numerology number is a one.
That's right, my baby is just like daddy!
Y'all couldn't shut me up never, I always spoke my mind,
in love with the world, like my brother with caddies.
Shine your glow lil mama, do not let anything stop you.
God himself got a plan for you.
Grab a dictionary and find your name and think about it,
then, take a deep breath and do what you gotta do.

*Do your thing baby girl,
speak to the world, justice is for all.*

Our Moon

Dedicated to: Mama J

From the most talented woman that I have ever met,
Along with a militant bloodline, conceived the wonderful Janette.
On two twenty two, nineteen fifty three, time changed.
Due to the fact of the most pure heart became.

Being one of the pair, of the un-identical twins,
Made them the middle children of six, with parallel lives until the end.
God bless her soul, her twin passed in two thousand and two.
Our moon lost a major part of her, and I did too.

Thou she's so strong, she continued to go on.
With, a shine shown from every dust to dawn.
Amazingly designed, so proud she mothered mines.
Me being the middle of five siblings,
Like her, placed me, right on time.

An abnormal moon you are, because, you forever stay full.
Staying in charge of our orders, like the red sighted by bulls.
I cannot see you leaving before me.
I am just an apple of your tree.
I know for sho, our moon, throughout eternity,
will remain legendary.

We Love U 4 Ever Big Mama J

To Be Better Than

Dedicated to: my Popz

I never had a chance to sit down with you and talk.
We never had a father to son understanding.
Thou my Love for you is indescribable,
we deserve a better bondage, on that note,
that's what I'm demanding.
It was hard being raised by a mother to be a man,
so, indeed the streets took hold,
molding the shape of me.
I don't fault you for disappearing,
I've learned to live with regrets, pops,
I made it to be the best I could be.
Let us start Love over, making a difference with life,
let us treat our bloodline with royalty.
Let us liberate the status of the evildoer marriage,
and behold, found strength in our loyalty.
What a family to be, such a team full of stars,
with you being the coach, leading us to the top.
With strong blood cells being created daily, due to bad pressure,
Relieved, there's just no way that our circle could be stop.
Let's strive to do better than our past, our present is settled,
which, can only lead to a joyful future.
Respecting ourselves no matter what,
keeping our guard up on hate,
visualizing our days to come mature.
The best thing about our relationship, is that we still got a chance,
we can't give up, God don't like no quitters.
The Lord is an over-standing being, Loving to help us rise,
so, once we've prayed, he'll be sure to forgive us sliders.
Time to see it from my view, yap the time is now,
we are, "free at last, free at last, free at last."
Making the best of situations with the time,
we got left, slowing it down, and no more living it fast.
I made you a Grandfather, yea I got kids of my own,
and it's a must, I raise them better than the way I grew.
Of course, the aim is to be better than yesterday,
so, lets let the Love circulate through what's left of the Taylor crew.

Mr. Relentless

Dedicated to: Ian (N.E. Mac)

Off the top! Nonstop! It is I – Mr. Relentless!
It's like no matter, whatever I get started, I never ends it.
Call me the run on sentence with no period.
Yea I'm a Nigga, but, far from being ignorant.

My rhymes stampede minds, like saints marching.
My computerized memory, stay sharp like ironed starching.
O you likes, like Ray Charles, well A Ha! I got another one.
Said, who's hotter than me, Ha! It got to be the sun.

Over the top and beyond, I manifested my actions.
I asked, believed, then received, because nothing just happens.
In another location, calling shots, like I'm their captain.
Still getting my hustle, on with these words, I'm steady trapping.

I'm the relentless lyricist, constantly spitting the realest hits.
I take a track out of nothing, then making something another hit.
When opportunity glances, I will advance on the chart list.
Initiating myself, as the nations number one artist.
This is far from the start; I truly define MC.
So, if there's anybody tighter than me,
Well, like TI, "You gonna need a track featuring Jesus and Jay Z."

The Left Be Hinder

Dedicated to: Logan

Brought in this world from a night full of lust,
from those who didn't wear a rubber, or either it bust.
I never met my moms; she was gone from the jump.
I wasn't able to stay with my dad, because, his life was so slumped.
Group homes and institutions, raised the wild in me.
I have skills to make it on my own, but, which style should it be.
I'm smarter than the average, but, I'm not Yogi.
I'm imprisoned with a marketing plan, waiting on my release.
I have nobody to call on, except for our Loving God.
I'm a indigent inmate, with no mail for me, being brought to my pod.
I denied my own bond, due to the lack of an address.
Praying for an inmate to come through, with help only leaves me stressed.
Why me? I often ask, hiding my pain behind a smile.
Why am I the left-be-hinder, with a stomach that always growls.
Can anybody who hears my silent cry, bring forth an open door for me?
One that leads to opportunity,
for, I can finally have a chance at my Liberty.
I'm not ashamed of who I am, I'm just waiting patiently to exhale.
Lost in a nation full of sin, searching for heaven, dwelling in hell.

Pray for me.

You Lost One

Dedicated to: Weak Links

Funny, how tables turn in the blink of an eye,
                  going from top dawg to small guy.
Better to be feared than Loved, is what I should've shown,
                  instead of trying to give Love a try.
How could y'all switch like a trick, leaving me solo in the mix,
                  thought it was all for one, and one for all.
I got locked behind walls, and the light broke night.
                  Fake niggas ain't even answered my calls.
Ain't even send no money to my books, not a letter to read,
                  nor a picture to help me vent through the flames.
Such a shame, when I was Always there for y'all.
No, I can't be the one to blame.

I was told,
    the best way to get back at people, is basically, to just truly ignore them.
It's a thin line, between Love and hate,
                  soon as they get to saying, "I Love you."
That's when you find out, you wish you never had known them.
Don't even bother to explain, my feelings won't change,
                  I'm starting to hate y'all boys with a passion.
No it ain't,
    "You came up with them niggas huh, you stuck with them niggas huh,"
                  because, dawg, shit got drastic.
Nope, I ain't throwing bricks hiding my hand.
I lays it bluntful, Mr. Foney, I never been your fan.
But, it's time for me to switch the subject,
                  because, y'all ain't worth my time.
So, ketchup and mustard when you can.

They Got Me Mad

Dedicated to: Crooked COs

First of all, my master is God, so, I'ma slave for him and him only.
Whatever he tells me to do, is what I'll do.
                              So, if you ain't him, you is a phony.
Don't give me no order to do, you can do yourself,
                                        unless you trying to pay me.
Tell you one thing, I ain't doing shit for free, you better reconsider,
                              because, ain't no trying to play me.

Don't take my kindness for a joke, because, I keep a smile on my face.
I'm trying to maintain my cool, treating all equal,
                              while, y'all steady hating my race.
Remember this, God got warriors.
So, one day I'll be in power above you.
With no mercy for your soul, as I watch you perish,
                        rotting in hell, while I'll be so sky blue.

                What
                        Goes
                                Around,
                                        Comes
                                                Around
                                                        Thou.

R.I.P. Fam

Rest in peace, Auntie Annette, I miss you dearly.
Rest in peace, Granny, Mrs. Holloway, you seen me as an atheist, but,
                                        I was only acting silly.
Rest in peace, Sammy and Samantha,
                        I wish, I would've got to known y'all better.
Ayo, PeeDee! Thinking of you, makes me mourn forever.
Ms. Sherry and Ms. Betty, it hurts to see y'all gone, already.
My Granny, Mrs. Justice, you never heard me call you Grandma,
                                but, it's Grandma daily.
R.I.P. LB and CP, I know y'all still watching over me.
Ayo, Dre!,
        I beg and pray, for one more day we can roll up and pass the tree.
My brethren Cedd Rocc, you taught me well,
                        and, a positive route, is what I now seek.
Rest in peace, my friend Lonny.
I'll never overstand, how you Loved me, more than your wifey.
Nigee', the young G,
                may you rest in peace, the haters took you a little too early.
I miss u Rudy, Lord knows, I wish you was here ,to sing my hooks,
                        smoking a fatty, while we stick them a birdie.
Big Daddy Bull, I'll never forget what you told me.
                I'm still the North star, holding the strength of the hood.
And, Yo Kenta! Everyday, is still your day.
                I can still see you smiling, saying, "It's all to the good."

Love and see y'all again.

Chapter 3
The Mind of The Heart

A Wounded Heart

Agony O'Agony, if only it could speak, that is what it would say.
Why is it I, that is constantly, and daily put to the test,
                                    as much as, I Love to pray?
Is it not I, that will lend, before I selfishly spend,
                                    on those, that I will forever care for?
Is it I, who has left the gates of the kingdom wide open,
                        when, there was nothing but a door closed?
I've introduced joy to misery, then misery to joy, then joy to misery, again.
I've had friends, turn into enemies, and in a matter of time,
                                    enemies turned into friends.
I bleed uncontrollably, literally, physically, and emotionally.
In need of a cure, for this internal suffering,
                        since, most would not even notice me.
I've been worn on shoulders, trampled by soldiers,
                        plus, stabbed from the front to the back.
I have fought with relatives, without regrets,
                                    but, now I wish to take it all back.
It hurts to think, it's the reason, I search the drink,
                                    and, smoke to ease the pain.
To live, Love, and laugh, is a beautiful thing.
                So, where's the umbrella for my pouring rain?
It's not hard to see that I'm scarred, as can be,
                        with a lot of lost Love, for the human ways.
Trying not to give up on faith, before the end of the days,
                        in order to remain with a smile on my face.
They buried a heart at Wounded Knee,
                        for the world to speak of manifest destiny.
If his story is "History," then let it be known with the truth,
                                    because, this is the life of me.

She Comes and Goes

Is it meant for me, to be alone, or not?
I have strived, to find that one, giving it all I got.
I've met a lot, and most of all, Ms. Hot to Trot,
and the ones that was down, still showed me doubts.

Then the day came, I found trust in the 'One' I found.
The connection was pure, we both loved being homebound.
But, it never fails, when involved, they all want me now,
and, with me living in sin, how could I turn them down.

Now, the "One" that was around, done packed up and gone.
I can't blame her for leaving, I treated that girl wrong.
So, now I'm back in search, for that One, hoping we'll get along.
Is it Izza?
Or, all around the world,
it's the same old song?

Love is Pain

You can't toy with Love, because people take it to the heart.
Be Smart.
It starts with a sweet feeling, until, it flames out like a spark.
It's Marked.
It's a curse, Adam and Eve, left on Earth for us.
It's No Trust.
Love comes in sexual healings, then walks out on lust.
Why Fuss?
I need a friend, to help me smooth these roads.
No Jokes.
Just strictly, friends, I cannot Love no mo.
For Sho.
I'll let it go, before I murk myself.
My Health.
Have to stay cool, before I cause my death.
She Left.
So, I'ma always think of someone else.
It Hurts.
I've tried to move on, but, it just don't work.
The Pain.
It's not natural, I put my Love in the dirt.
It's Buried.
Love is Pain and it's definitely scary.

Unnecessary Space

Sad to say, but, it is what it is, the fatherless child lives life.
The mother chooses to get aid,
                            from those, who hate on the father to have rights.
From birth, they approach the mother, with confusing questions,
                            without consent from the pops.
From that moment, she signed the government to help,
                            the mother and father's relationship stops.

There is nothing in the world, like a father raising his son,
                            and, more importantly, his girl.
Quality times' needed, not just Love from a distance,
                            especially, when she is my little girl.
To miss the times of crawling around, to walking and crying,
                            all day to talking, it is what you call true hurt.
The years of no memory, kills the father from stress,
                            all because, of how the system works.

Now, as the time goes by, and the mother moves on,
                            the father will find himself in court.
Due to the "Jim Crow" syndrome, in the females dome,
                            placing the father on child support.
He tries his best to pay his dues, but, jobs just isn't enough.
Coming up short by the week, until the weeks turn into months,
                            to doing time behind cash and cuffs.

Decades have passed, and nothing has changed,
                            the mother and the father is doing the same.
What a waste of time, when they could have stayed together doing fine,
                            teaching the kids to walk through the rain.
Now the babies are older, and at the point in life,
                            where they themselves, are out having kids.
Without knowledge of a family staying together,
                            they will nine times out of ten, live out the same bids.

Way The Love At?

Call me the Provider of the circle I rump with.
Yea, I'm the go getter, the brain of the operation of our hustling click.
Being there for whatever the cause, for my dawgz, I'll break the laws.
But,will they all do the same for me?
                        Because, I'm seeing some doing not at all.

I went half on a baby with those, so called ladies, thou they're so shady.
Throwing me to the vultures, and on top of that,
                        not even letting me raise my own babies.
Can I even get a picture? And, why are you letting them hit?
                        Are they the new now daddies of my jits?
I'm trying to hold the cursing back, but, where is the Love at?
                        Said, y'all bitches ain't about shit!

And, when I'm locked up in a jail, with money waiting on me out there,
                        where, in the world, is my family at?
A lawyer said, he can get me back home for two stacks.
                        And, y'all ain't even trying to give him that.

Is there even Love, still in this world to give,
                        or, are we all just caught up in sin?
I've played my part, on numerous occasions,
                        but, still find myself alone in a lion's den.
And, now that I've visualized to realize, I know just where the Love is at.
It's trapped in my heart, waiting on its release date,
                        and, that day is when I'll see the pearly gates.
Because, God is, the only one that's one hundred percent... Got my back!

Don't Play Yourself

She's everything you want, she's everything you need.
She's your definition of the word, which spells L.O.V.E.
From the quality times spent together, she's hard to ever let go.
Thou spiritually, mentally, or physically,
                          she's everything you need and mo.

She's your wife to be, the mother of your kids,
                          your Moonish reflection of you.
Your significant other, your soul mate and Lover,
                          your uplift, when days are blue.
She loves you forever, today and tomorrow, her heart belongs to you.
Her mind and body, is yours to keep, but, her soul belongs to God,
                          which, is cool.
At times, it gets rough,
      dealing with the emotional roller coaster, we all must witness.
Faith only comes with a test, which, never stops questioning,
                          so, stay strong along the mission.
There come times for break ups, but, we are only human,
                          daily living by flesh.
But, break ups lead to stronger make ups, when the Love is true.
                          So, continue to see yourself so blessed.

Don't get off track, if separation appears,
                          believe, when I say she'll never go astray.
You've heard it before, "If you Love something, let it go,
                          if it comes back to you, then it's yours to stay."
So, make a manly choice, and hold down the court,
                          because, family matters, no matter what's the course.
Don't play yourself, by giving up, because, God don't like quitters.
Remember, Real Love doesn't end with divorce.

It's till death do y'all apart,
so, let patience work her perfection.

One Day At A Time

I think about you often, and it makes me smile.
Just the sight of you in my mind, is worth the while.
I have been patient, waiting for someone, to share my joy with.
Indeed, in need of a true friend, to spend some quality time with.
Such a hard working person I am, truly blessed and honest.
Willing to show you better than I can tell you,
instead of making a promise.
I am the best cook, and a great massager.
Ready to hand you unlimited smiles, so trust, I'll never dodge you.
I can be a father figure, if you accept my holla.
I'll place you before me in my days, so my pride, I'll swallow.
We can plan better tomorrows, making sure they'll shine.
But, to see this friendship flow smooth, lets just take it one day at a time.

The slow lane passion.

Soothing Suzy

How do I Love thee, let me count the ways.
I'm such an admirer of your desirable tastes.
Just the thought of you alone, often makes me mourn.
You're the lift of my frowns, at times, when I'm forlorn.
O Suzy, O Suzy, How do I Love thee?
Such a precious sight you are, so Lovely and sexy.
You are a charm, a delight, a choice one must choose.
Ms. Suzy is a pleaser, and her job is to soothe.
You take my mind off the world, when my drive is drowsy.
I'll never dress you lousy, thou, you leave my vision cloudy.
No, I'm not mad, at how you get passed around the circle.
As long as, you continue to support your favorite color, purple.
Ms. Soothing Suzy, you really blow my mind.
It is you, my Love, whom keeps my motive in line?

She activates my thought process.

Sweet Memories

When all the games are done and played,
and, the night won't turn back into day.
When the light has faded away,
and, my sight has seen no way.
When the body is over,
and, the party is over.
When the time has come,
and, I will not get any older.
All we'll have is,
those sweet memories.
When your Love ones meditate,
on the times, when y'all would celebrate.
When their cries won't hesitate, to travel south, upon their face.
When today, will not turn back into yesterday.
When tomorrow, could never be, without living through today.
When all is left, is just the thought of the days.
We will behold those sweet memories, confirming that every thing's okay.

The sweetness of remembrance.

Chapter 4
My Biblical Sight

U Choose

I'm losing my religion slowly, this world is killing me softly.
I'm in Love with the higher being, but, the devil won't get up off me.
I'm very loquacious in prayer, begging one day, I take it there,
to a heavenly state of mind, up until then, I'm trapped in here.
Here, being the body, the temple, the house,
containing both good and evil, with the free will to choose my route.
Day in, day out, I fight against this everlasting battle.
Seeing myself with wings one moment, then the next with a rattle.
My soul is on fire, yet my minds at peace.
I'm bamming with the beast, as I stand at ease.
I'm on my knees, with my palms, parallel to each other.
Putting in a Hail Mary, getting tempted by the devil.
U must choose your destiny, is what something keeps telling me.
Just can't play both sides of the fence, because, lukewarm ain't what it be.
I have to make a firm decision, and I gotta make it now.
Because, I can't tell if I'll wake up after laying it down.
And, this one goes out to the ever-dominant creature,
in this game of life we play, the song will only be performed as a solo,
and not, as a full feature!

The Broken Leg

For the Lord is my Shepherd, I shall not want.
Through him, all is possible if asked, and, then doing is nothing he won't.
Carry me, my Father, for my leg is broken.
I'm the lost sheep, seeking home, through these prayers spoken.
Please enlighten my darkness, take me from here to there.
I have a passionate soul, thou, it often grew without a care.
I'm a sinner, whom have sinned, but, in your name I declare.
A change to make, in order to dwell, with you forever in the air.
Tote these bags of burdens, my Lord, relieve my soul from the hurt,
For the long suffering of you is salvation,
so, forever for you, I'll put in work.
I'll grow in grace, as you GPS my walk, toward your light.
Loving the fellowship, we've bound, being cleansed from all sins,
through, Jesus Christ.
Allow me a spot and position, in your kingdom,
making me a new addition.
It's a constant battle with the negative, for me, but, through you,
it's no competition.
As I, witness you, making it disappear like a magician,
I'll strive to have it all on one accord, signing this new petition.
I am your Chief Musician, speaking Savior unto the youth,
as if, you commanded me to grant all of your wishes.

My soul belongs to you my lord.

The Power Of Prayer

The more corruption to the system,
the lesser the reception,
toward the power of the prayer.

Trapped In The Belly

There is a reason, I am here, I should have played my part.
I chose to go astray, being all selfish with God.
Ignored the chores he gave, knowing I am his slave.
Delivering messages, through the body, until the time of my grave.

So, here I am in the beast, still alive with abilities.
With no way to run, no way to hide, I'm forced to learn to set peace.
While being a positive energy, I wait in constant prayer.
Now knowing, not to fear my destiny, because, my Lord is there.

Whatever is out there, for me to reach and teach,
I'll teach wherever I explore.
Traveling the lands, to save souls, once I'm spit back out on the shore.
Praising God for my learnings, for I do now, whatever he tells me.
Such an experience I have witnessed, being trapped off in the belly.

The Disciple

I do walk in the light of the Lord, outlasting the darkness there was.
Learning how to become a teacher of the word,
$\qquad\qquad\qquad$ to go around, sharing the Love.
I do hate sin, but, Love the sinners, and even I myself sin daily.
In Love with the world, no matter how bad, they treat themselves,
$\qquad\qquad\qquad$ I will strive not to be shady.

Once his chores are given, I'll remain his slave,
$\qquad\qquad\qquad$ and, he'll remain my master.
I will spiritually be a part of his heavenly body,
$\qquad\qquad\qquad$ once the world burns from the disasters.

My Lord, I'm here for whatever your cause,
$\qquad\qquad\qquad$ saving souls along my journey.
Taking care of your business, you left me, because,
$\qquad\qquad\qquad$ I am in him, as he, is in me.

Please lord tell me what to do.

Word of the Day

Confirmational joy, is such a feeling to behold.
The rejoicer is gratefully sought, restoration is in thy soul.
It brings forth no more hurt, just wonderful days.
The savior mentioned, all the righteous ways.
It seeks no confusion, its habitation is now forever.
Delivered on time like Pizza Hut, making the hope and trust better.
It took me out of the hand of the wicked, preparing me for everlasting life,
                    molding me into a wonder unto many,
                          as I, praise thee Father, with all thy might.
It's a lively smile, in all of the days of salvation to come.
It gives you the courage to go forward,
                          no matter where you are coming from.
It allows the chance to die, old and gray headed,
                          showing strength unto this generation.
It's the work of God, who has done all great things,
                                known as the anti-abomination.
The word of the day is, the news of the being, of the sinful flesh fulfilling.
It's simply said, rarely lead, but, it is what it is,
                          and, this word is known as, Redemption.

The Devil's Plot

From the moment he rebelled, being against God's will,
        being thrown out of the heavens above.
He found himself a home, going to and from,
        manipulating those of the Earth, full of passionate love.
Doing all that he can, until his time is up, speaking,
        "respite me until they are raised."
"They," being us, lost in a world full of lust,
        making it harder to awake and give God praise.
His hobby is to collect souls, he loves getting at God's faithful servants,
        so, please keep an eye open for him.
His goals are to destroy his foes, and he's at work daily,
        so, forever we must continue to ignore him.
It's not going to be easy, and, it's not suppose to be.
Our Father, allows him to test our faith,
        and, no matter what he takes from us, never question God why,
        for the Lord'll giveth back, more than he'll take.
The fallen angel, and his empire use people,
        trying his best to leave us in a carnal mind.
Be of the spirit, not of the flesh, release yourself from his grip,
        and, do your best not to slip to his kind.
He has no shine, no kids, no fortunes to give that will last,
        and, no Real Love for God's world, and since he can't create,
        his only chance is to trick and accumulate the men,
        women, boys, and girls.
Beware, of the ghost, no matter what people tell you,
        talking about what you don't see, won't hurt you.
He owns a misery show, and, he keeps looking for new stars to be on it,
        and, his show goes on with no commercials.
We can't defeat him at all, because it's not our job or purpose,
        the only thing we can do is rebuke him.
Remember, he's moving faster than how he used to be,
        getting at ALL, because his time of being is slim.

Stay Out of His Reach,
Because the Block is Hot!

Get Your Hand Out of My Pocket

In the beginning, God created the Heavens and the Earth, from the thoughts of his very loving heart. Such a mystery on how, such a mystery on why, but, never a mystery on was he smart? It took him six days of work, and one day of rest, which he blessed, and called it the Sabbath. "And he saw that it was good," for everyday that he worked, while the evil was waiting, patiently plotting on how to inhabit. And, with man he made in his own image, to be fruitful, multiply, and replenish. From the herbs yielding seed, from the fruit trees yielding fruit, he said "thy shall be used for meat throughout thy living. And, in this Garden of Eden, where Adam was placed, forever so happy to be. He was given charge over the animals, but, God noticed his loneliness and therefore he created Eve. And, there in the midst of the garden, stood a tree of knowledge of good and evil, forbidden to neither touch nor eat of. Along with a conning serpent, so beguiled with his ways, with a plan to destroy the true meaning of love. And, as its thoughts proceeded, it met up with Eve in the midst of the garden, near the tree. Persuading her to touch and eat from it, as she did, becoming as gods, knowing good and evil, with open eyes to who we be. Curse thy face of the Lord, did Adam and Eve do, and for sure was soon to be punished. Settled for consequences, and definitely stood defenseless, to the charming minds ungarnished. With wrong being committed, they were cast out of the garden, with new standards on the ways they will be living. Throwing away a great bit of god's intentions, he had done already laid out for our everlasting living. Simple is, as simple read, as simple said, as simple as that. As I said before, and I'll tell Satan again, "You need to get cho--boy, you need to get back!" God's will, will happen, he is the director of his movie he is watching. With us being his children, we must carry out our duties, with no pausing and certainly no stopping. There are two lanes to the game, the good and the evil, and they both are offered for free. However, abusing what is meant, and riding with the wrong, shall thy perish and never again be. You see, Satan and his angels have been on the prowl, from day one, and more welcomed in the heart, nowadays. With our new generation of babies, being his major targets, it's as if they're being taught, from birth to go astray. Blessed is he, that can hold his own, while also honoring thy mother and thy father. Continuing to tell the devil at every second that he try, "Man, I'm not trying to be bothered!" See, with thoughts like that, there's Jesus in your heart, the ransom for all human needs. Granting us an opened door to heaven, basically, by taking your time to sit down and read. From hiding, the devil has been released, just a singing and tap dancing away in the streets. Even lounging on couches, in the households of annointers, just as happy as he ever possibly can be. But, with this soul that I am blessed with, a soul given from the gulf of heaven, I must strive to take flight like a rocket. Teaching all what I have learned to those full of questions, advising all to tell that devil to...

Get your hand out of my pocket.

Until They Are Raised

And, Satan said, "Respite me until they are raised."
"They," being the children of men,
              who lost their knowledge, from their beginning days.
And, God allowed Satan his time of trickery,
                            causing souls to commit blasphemy.
With knowing his time is ending, he is full blast with sending,
                            wolves to dress in sheeps' clothing.
God's plan for us, is to smarten up in a rush, praising with grace,
                                    steady living in faith.
We the people, must open our minds, and rise above hatred,
                        in order to have the wicked erased.
Let us now, all together, all on one accord,
                    modify the sinful ways in our lives.
Joining forces to end the heavenly wars,
                    that natural eyes, don't see in the skies.

United with Faith in God,
We Shall Stand Forever.

Touched by an Angel

Who are these people, where did they come from?
I must ask, why is it that they come to me?
Am I that special to be confronted by these special people,
Teaching me more about our G.O.D.?
I knew somehow, I would play a part in your role,
to reach out to our upcoming generations.
Help them give themselves a chance to save their souls,
before they reclassify for the Kingdom of Satan.
Father, I'm thankful for all that you do for me,
Especially, at times of distress, when I really need help.
When I can depend on no man, it's always you with a Helping hand,
revealing my already made plan to rep.
Then you send good people that I encounter with,
Making me feel great about living out our daily bread.
Teaching me to perform "Miracles" like Jesus feeding
the many people with two fish and five loaves of bread.
There's a learning process that we all go through.
Dealing with the fact that we are all born with sin.
Being touched by knowledge to having an understanding of wisdom,
Is what gives forever life after the body ends.
I often asked where was my angel to please, when I was down and out?
Because, growing up was quite rough.
But, there was never a time you placed more on me I couldn't bare,
Sparing my rebuking with Lucifer to be just.
Is it you moving my hand on this paper my lord?
Is it you giving me those beautiful words to write?
It's just no coincidence for this talent I posses in my heart.
Is it that I now learn to walk with Christ?
Whatever's clever, I'm with it, no matter which way you want to go,
and no matter what it is that you want me to do.
I've been touched by an angel and now I must return the blessing,
Touching those in need of the same taught truth.

Peace Be Still

No matter how troublesome life will seem, it is going to be okay.
Jesus will fix all our problems, come Judgment Day.
Just keep the faith and patience, while waiting, for the day he returns.
Relaxation, cool, calm, and collected, is what we should yearn.
Thou the devil, can make situations, like a rowboat in a hurricane.
Tossing us around, and throwing us off course, when the madness rains.
But, believing in Christ in prayer, shall he lead thy ways.
Allowing peace to be still, once "peace be still," is what he'll say.

Through Jesus, All is Possible.

Author

Mr. Leroyce, was born in the small city of Aiken, South Carolina, in 1980, an area known for it's retirement community, seeking a slower life. Yes, an 80's baby. He was the middle child of five, raised by a single mom in a single parent household, in what society called "the projects."

Mr. Leroyce, grew up in poverty for a couple of decades which only made him stronger. Coming from a community full of unfit ways, gave him the insight to be "better than," once grown. Inspired by "Street Knowledge," though textbook smart too, is what gave him his natural style to shine.

With the greatest decision he ever made, he decided to "Each One, Reach One, Teach One," through one of his favorite talents; poetry. Through it, he was enlightened to be enlightened consistently, throughout the good and the bad times, no matter what it took or continues to take for him to do that. With his positive aim, yet foggy past, he boldly stands for change with great passion, bringing it to you raw and uncut, as an overseer. With a confident insight, he delivers harmony to "One Nation," with the heart of leadership. He strives to be a symbol for justice and to remain loyal to the truth.

Family

Lightning Source UK Ltd.
Milton Keynes UK
UKHW010650211119
353936UK00003B/119/P